EPI DIET COOKBOOK FOR BEGINNERS 2024

A Complete Beginner's Guide to Managing Exocrine Pancreatic Insufficiency with Custom Food Lists, Low-Fat Recipes and a Strategic Meal Plan

Dr. NAOMI WOOD

TABLE OF CONTENT

Acknowledgement

As I reflect on the journey of creating this book, my heart is filled with gratitude and appreciation. First and foremost, I would like to thank my family. Your support, patience, and encouragement have been the foundation upon which this book was built. To my spouse, who endured countless taste tests and late-night writing sessions, your love and understanding mean the world to me. To my children, whose curiosity and joy remind me of the importance of health and wellness, thank you for being my inspiration.

Thank you, friends, for being my biggest supporters. Your honest feedback and belief in this project have kept me motivated and focused.

I am deeply grateful to the health and wellness community. To the nutritionists, dietitians, and health experts who shared their knowledge and insights, your guidance has been invaluable. Your dedication to promoting healthy living has inspired me to create a book that is not only informative but also accessible and practical.

To you, reader of this book, thanks for starting this journey with me. Your enthusiasm and dedication to improve your health and well-being are what make this work worthwhile. I hope that the recipes and information within these pages inspire you to live your healthiest, happiest life.

Every page of this book is a reflection of the love and collaborative support I have received. My heart is full of gratitude, and I am honored to share this work with you.

Thank you from the bottom of my heart.

Introduction

I still remember the day I discovered the Epi Diet. It was a rainy afternoon, and I was frustrated by my health. I had tried countless diets, each promising miracles but all ended in disappointment. Lisa, my friend, had invited me over for lunch.

As I stepped into her kitchen, the aroma of freshly prepared food filled the air. She served me a colorful plate of grilled vegetables, quinoa salad, and a delicious smoothie. It wasn't just delicious; it also made me feel light and energized. Lisa smiled and replied, *"It's an Epi Diet."* *"You should try it!"*

That meal marked the beginning of a life-changing journey. The Epi Diet isn't just another fad; it's a path to a healthier, more vibrant life. It's about nourishing your body with wholesome, natural foods that are rich in nutrients and low in empty calories. But more than that, it's about transforming your relationship with food, learning to enjoy every bite while fueling your body for optimal health.

When you start the Epi Diet, you're not just making a temporary change. You're embarking on a journey that can reshape your life. This diet focuses on whole, unprocessed foods that support your overall well-being. It's about eating a variety of fruits, vegetables, lean proteins, and whole grains. It's about choosing foods that are close to their natural state, avoiding those laden with artificial additives and preservatives.

One of the most beautiful aspects of the Epi Diet is how it encourages **mindfulness**. It teaches you to listen to your body and recognize its signals of hunger and fullness. Instead of counting calories or obsessing over portion sizes, you learn to savor your meals, appreciating the flavors and textures. This mindful approach helps you develop a healthier, more positive relationship with food.

Starting this journey might seem daunting at first, especially if you're used to the convenience of processed foods. However, keep in mind that every step you take is one closer to becoming a healthier person. Begin by making small changes. Swap out sugary snacks for fresh fruit. Replace refined grains with whole grains. Gradually, these small changes will add up, and you'll start to notice the difference in how you feel.

As you follow the Epi Diet, you'll discover a world of delicious, satisfying meals that nourish your body while also pleasing your taste buds. You'll find joy in cooking and experimenting with new recipes. You'll notice improvements in your energy, emotions, and overall health. Most importantly, you will understand that healthy eating does not have to be restrictive or boring. It can be a wonderful and rewarding experience.

This cookbook is your companion on this journey. It's filled with recipes designed to make the Epi Diet easy and enjoyable. From hearty breakfasts to satisfying dinners, from quick snacks to indulgent desserts, you'll find a wide variety of options to suit your tastes and lifestyle. Each recipe is crafted to provide maximum nutrition with minimal effort, so you can spend less time in the kitchen and more time enjoying your meals.

So, welcome to the Epi Diet journey. Accept it with an open heart and adventurous spirit. Remember that the goal is to make progress rather than perfection. Celebrate each healthy choice you make and learn from any setbacks. Have patience with yourself and have faith in the process. You are transforming your life, not just changing your diet.

Here's to a healthier, happier you.

1
What is Epi Diet?

Imagine a life where food not only satisfies your hunger but also fuels your body, mind, and spirit. This is the promise of the Epi Diet, a lifestyle choice that goes beyond mere eating. It's a way of embracing health, vitality, and happiness through the foods we choose to nourish ourselves with.

The Epi Diet is built on a foundation of simple, whole foods. These are foods that are as close to their natural state as possible, unprocessed and unrefined. Think of fresh fruits and vegetables, lean proteins, whole grains, nuts, and seeds. These foods are rich in the nutrients our bodies need to thrive, without the harmful additives that can weigh us down.

At its heart, the Epi Diet is about balance and variety. It is not necessary to avoid certain food groups or adhere to rigid regulations. Instead, it encourages you to eat a diverse range of foods that provide a variety of nutrients.

This variety ensures that your body gets everything it needs to function at its best. It's about eating the rainbow – incorporating different colored fruits and vegetables into your meals to get a diverse range of vitamins and minerals.

One of the key principles of the Epi Diet is **mindfulness**. In today's fast-paced world, it's easy to eat on the go and scarcely notice what we are eating. The Epi Diet invites you to slow down and truly appreciate your food. It motivates you to be conscious during meals, savoring each bite and paying attention to your body's signals of hunger and fullness. This mindful approach helps us to develop a healthier relationship with food, one that is based on enjoyment and respect rather than guilt and restriction.

The Epi Diet also emphasizes the importance of hydration. Water is necessary for every function in our bodies, including digestion, circulation, and temperature regulation. Drinking plenty of water throughout the day helps to keep our bodies running smoothly. Herbal teas and infusions can also be a wonderful addition, providing not only hydration but also additional nutrients and flavors.

Another important aspect of the Epi Diet is the idea of eating seasonally and locally whenever possible. Seasonal foods are the most flavorful and nutritious meals. They are also more likely to be fresher and less expensive. Eating locally supports your local economy and reduces the environmental impact of transporting food over long distances. It also allows you to connect more with the foods you eat and the people around you.

The Epi Diet encourages the inclusion of healthy fats in your diet. These are fats derived from avocados, almonds, seeds, and olive oil. They are essential for brain health, hormone production, and the absorption of certain vitamins. Unlike unhealthy fats found in processed foods, healthy fats can actually help to reduce inflammation and support overall health.

Proteins are another crucial component of the Epi Diet.

They are the building blocks of our bodies, necessary for repairing tissues, producing enzymes, and supporting a healthy immune system.

The Epi Diet recommends eating lean protein sources such as fish, poultry, beans, and legumes. It also encourages moderation when it comes to red meat and processed meats, which can have negative effects on health when consumed in excess.

Carbohydrates are not the enemy in the Epi Diet. Instead, it's about choosing the right carbs. Whole grains, fruits, and vegetables include complex carbs that give long-lasting energy and are high in fiber. Fiber is crucial for a healthy digestive system and can help control blood sugar levels.

Finally, the Epi Diet is about enjoyment and sustainability. It's neither a quick fix nor a temporary solution. It's a way of eating that you can maintain for life. It allows for flexibility and indulgence, understanding that food is not just fuel but also a source of pleasure and connection. It's about finding joy in cooking and eating, and about making choices that support your long-term health and well-being.

The Science Behind Epi Diet

The Epi Diet is not just another diet fad; it's grounded in solid science that aims to transform your health from the inside out. At its core, the Epi Diet focuses on eating whole, unprocessed foods that provide the essential nutrients our bodies need to function optimally. This approach is backed by numerous scientific studies that highlight the benefits of a nutrient-rich diet for overall well-being.

The concept of nutrient density is a key scientific principle behind the Epi Diet. Nutrient-dense foods are those that provide a high amount of vitamins, minerals, and other essential nutrients relative to their calorie content. These foods are typically whole and unprocessed, such as fruits, vegetables, lean proteins, and whole grains. By prioritizing these foods, the Epi Diet ensures that every bite you take is packed with the nutrients your body needs to thrive.

Research has shown that diets rich in fruits and vegetables are associated with a lower risk of chronic diseases, including heart disease, diabetes, and certain cancers. These plant-based foods are high in fiber, antioxidants, and phytochemicals, which work together to reduce inflammation and oxidative stress in the body. Fiber, in particular, plays a crucial role in digestive health by promoting regular bowel movements and supporting a healthy gut microbiome.

The gut microbiome is a fascinating area of study that has gained significant attention in recent years. It refers to the trillions of microorganisms living in our digestive tract, which play a vital role in our overall health. A diet rich in fiber from fruits, vegetables, and whole grains supports a diverse and healthy gut microbiome. This diversity is important because it helps to maintain a strong immune system, regulate metabolism, and even influence our mood and mental health.

Another key aspect of the Epi Diet is its focus on healthy fats. Unlike the unhealthy trans fats and saturated fats found in many processed foods, healthy fats from sources like avocados, nuts, seeds, and olive oil provide numerous health benefits. These fats are essential for brain health, hormone production, and the absorption of fat-soluble vitamins such as vitamins A, D, E, and K. Fatty fish and flaxseeds contain Omega-3 fatty acids, which have been shown to reduce inflammation and improve heart health.

Proteins are the building blocks of our bodies, and the Epi Diet emphasizes the importance of choosing lean sources of protein. Proteins from sources like fish, poultry, beans, and legumes provide the essential amino acids our bodies need for the growth, repair, and maintenance of tissues.

Additionally, these protein sources are often lower in saturated fats compared to red meat and processed meats, which are linked to an increased risk of chronic diseases when consumed in excess.

Carbohydrates are often misunderstood in many diets; however, they are embraced in the Epi Diet when they come from whole, unrefined sources. Whole grains, fruits, and vegetables provide complex carbohydrates that are digested more slowly, resulting in a steady release of energy and better blood sugar control. These foods are also rich in fiber, which helps to keep you feeling full and satisfied, reducing the likelihood of overeating.

The Epi Diet also emphasizes the importance of hydration. Water is essential for every function in our bodies, from digestion to temperature regulation to nutrient transport. Drinking enough water helps to keep our cells hydrated, supports kidney function, and aids in the elimination of toxins. Herbal teas and infusions can also contribute to our hydration needs while providing additional nutrients and flavors.

Another scientific principle behind the Epi Diet is the concept of eating seasonally and locally. Seasonal fruits are collected at their peak ripeness, resulting in greater freshness and nutrient density.

Local foods, which don't have to travel long distances to reach your plates, often retain more of their nutritional value. This approach not only supports your health but also benefits the environment by reducing the carbon footprint associated with transporting food.

Mindful eating is another cornerstone of the Epi Diet, supported by scientific research on the benefits of mindfulness practices. Mindful eating means paying close attention to the eating experience, savoring each bite, and responding to your body's hunger and fullness cues. According to studies, practicing mindful eating can help reduce overeating, improve digestion, and increase overall enjoyment of food. It encourages you to slow down and appreciate the flavors, textures, and aromas of your meals, fostering a deeper connection to the food you eat.

The Epi Diet's emphasis on whole, unprocessed foods also helps to reduce the intake of harmful substances found in many processed foods, such as added sugars, artificial additives, and unhealthy fats. These substances have been linked to a variety of health issues, including obesity, diabetes, heart disease, and even certain cancers. By avoiding these ingredients and focusing on natural, nutrient-dense foods, the Epi Diet supports long-term health and well-being.

Antioxidants play a significant role in the Epi Diet, as they help protect your cells from damage caused by free radicals. Free radicals are unstable molecules that can cause oxidative stress,

leading to inflammation and a higher risk of chronic diseases. Antioxidants, found abundantly in fruits, vegetables, nuts, and seeds, neutralize free radicals and help maintain cellular health. This protection is crucial for reducing the risk of diseases and promoting overall vitality.

The Epi Diet also incorporates the concept of glycemic index (GI), which measures how quickly a food raises blood sugar levels. Foods with a low GI, such as whole grains, legumes, and most fruits and vegetables, cause a slower and more gradual increase in blood sugar. It also helps prevent energy spikes and crashes, making keeping a consistent energy level all day easier. Managing blood sugar levels is essential for preventing diabetes and insulin resistance.

2
Ingredients and Tools

When you embark on the Epi Diet journey, the right ingredients and tools become your trusted companions. They make cooking an enjoyable and creative process, transforming simple foods into delicious, nourishing meals that support your health and well-being. Let's dive into the essentials that will set you up for success in your Epi Diet kitchen.

Essential Ingredients

1. Fresh Fruits and Vegetables: These are the heart and soul of the Epi Diet. Vibrant, colorful, and packed with nutrients, they provide the vitamins, minerals, and fiber your body needs. Think of juicy tomatoes, crisp bell peppers, leafy greens like spinach and kale, sweet berries, and refreshing citrus fruits. Each bite brings a burst of flavor and health benefits, making them indispensable in your diet.

2. Whole Grains: Whole grains like quinoa, brown rice, oats, and barley are excellent sources of complex carbohydrates and fiber. They keep you full and energized all day. These grains are unrefined, meaning they retain all their natural goodness, unlike processed grains that lose much of their nutritional value.

3. Lean Proteins: Proteins are essential for building and repairing tissues, and the Epi Diet encourages lean sources. Chicken breast, turkey, fish, beans, lentils, and tofu are all great options. These proteins provide the necessary amino acids without the unhealthy fats found in processed meats.

4. Healthy Fats: Not all fats are created equally. Healthy fats from avocados, nuts, seeds, and olive oil are vital for brain health, hormone production, and nutrient absorption. They also add a wonderful richness to your meals, making them more satisfying and delicious.

5. Nuts and Seeds: Almonds, walnuts, chia seeds, and flaxseeds are nutrient powerhouses. They're high in healthy fats, protein, and fiber. Sprinkling them on salads, yogurt, or oatmeal can enhance both the flavor and nutritional value of your dishes.

6. Herbs and Spices: These not only add flavor but also come with numerous health benefits. Turmeric, garlic, ginger, rosemary, basil, and cilantro can transform a simple meal into a culinary delight. They are high in antioxidants and anti-inflammatory properties, so each bite benefits your health.

7. Legumes: Beans, lentils, and chickpeas are fantastic sources of plant-based protein and fiber. They are incredibly versatile and can be used in soups, stews, salads, and even as a base for veggie burgers.

8. Dairy and Alternatives: For those who consume dairy, options like Greek yogurt, kefir, and low-fat cheese are excellent choices. If you prefer non-dairy alternatives, almond milk, coconut yogurt, and soy cheese are excellent substitutes, with similar textures and flavors.

Essential Tools

1) High-Quality Knives: A good set of knives is indispensable. Sharp, reliable knives make chopping fruits, vegetables, and meats quicker and safer. Purchase a chef's knife, a paring knife, and a serrated knife to meet all of your cutting needs.

2) **Cutting Boards:** Have separate cutting boards for vegetables and meats to avoid cross-contamination. Wooden or bamboo boards are durable and easy to clean, making them ideal for your kitchen.

3) **Blender and Food Processor:** These appliances are incredibly versatile. A blender is perfect for making smoothies, soups, and sauces, while a food processor can handle chopping, slicing, and grating tasks with ease.

4) **Non-Stick Cookware:** Non-stick pans and pots make cooking and cleanup easier. They require less oil, which is great for keeping your meals

healthy. Look for high-quality, long-lasting options that can withstand frequent use.

5) **Steamer Basket:** Steaming vegetables helps retain their nutrients and vibrant colors. A steamer basket is a simple tool that fits into most pots, allowing you to cook vegetables, fish, and even dumplings healthily.

6) **Baking Sheets and Parchment Paper:** For roasting vegetables, baking healthy snacks, or cooking lean proteins, baking sheets and parchment paper are essential. They help avoid sticking and make cleanup easier.

7) **Mixing Bowls:** A variety of mixing bowls in different sizes is crucial for preparing ingredients, mixing salads, or marinating meats. Stainless steel or glass

bowls are durable and easy to clean.

8) **Measuring Cups and Spoons:** Accurate measurements are key to consistent results, especially when baking or trying new recipes. A set of measuring cups and spoons ensures you use the right amounts of ingredients every time.

9) **Salad Spinner:** Fresh salads are a staple in the Epi Diet, and a salad spinner makes washing and drying greens quick and efficient. Dry greens hold onto dressings better, making your salads more flavorful.

10) **Spice Grinder or Mortar and Pestle:** Freshly ground spices have a more intense flavor compared to pre-ground ones. A spice grinder or a mortar and pestle allows you to grind your spices just before use, enhancing the taste of your dishes.

11) **Storage Containers:** A good set of storage containers makes it easier to organize your pantry and keep leftovers fresh. Choose glass containers, which are durable and don't absorb odors or stains.

12) **Colander:** Draining pasta, rinsing beans, or washing vegetables is more convenient with a sturdy colander. It helps you prep your ingredients quickly and efficiently.

13) **Immersion Blender:** For pureeing soups directly in the pot or making smoothies in a tall glass, an immersion blender is a handy tool. It saves time and reduces the number of dishes you need to wash.

14) **Kitchen Scale:** For precise measurements, especially when

baking or following specific dietary plans, a kitchen scale is invaluable. It ensures that your recipes are accurate and consistent.

Having these ingredients and tools at your disposal sets the stage for a successful and enjoyable Epi Diet experience. They enable you to prepare meals that are not only nutritious but also tasty and satisfying. Embrace the journey with these essentials, and you'll find that cooking becomes a joyful, nourishing activity that supports your overall well-being.

Tips for Beginners

Starting the Epi Diet can feel like stepping into a new world. It's exciting, but also overwhelming. Many have walked this path and found it to be a rewarding journey. Here are some tips to help you get started and stay motivated along the way.

1. Start Slow

Change doesn't have to happen overnight. Start by making tiny changes to your current diet. Change out one unhealthy snack for a piece of fruit or a handful of nuts. Replace processed grains with whole grains like quinoa or brown rice. Gradually eat more of fruits and veggies. Over time, small steps accumulate into large changes.

2. Plan Your Meals

Planning is your best friend when starting the Epi Diet. Set aside time every week to organize your meals. Write down what you'll eat for breakfast, lunch, dinner, and snacks. This helps you stay on track and makes grocery shopping easier. Plus, having a plan reduces the temptation to grab unhealthy convenience foods.

3. Keep It Simple

Don't feel like you need to create gourmet meals every day. Simple recipes with fresh, whole ingredients can be just as delicious and satisfying. A fresh salad with a variety of vegetables, a lean protein like grilled chicken, and a drizzle of olive oil can be a perfect meal. Start with easy recipes and build your confidence in the kitchen.

4. Stock Your Kitchen

Having the right ingredients on hand makes it easier to stick to the Epi Diet. Fill your pantry with whole grains, beans, nuts, and seeds. Keep your fridge stocked with fresh fruits and vegetables, lean proteins, and healthy fats like avocados and olive oil. When healthy options are readily available, you're more likely to reach for them.

5. Hydrate, Hydrate, Hydrate

Water is essential for your body's functions. Make sure you drink plenty of water all day. Bring a reusable water bottle with you as a reminder to stay hydrated. Herbal teas and infused waters can also be great options to keep things interesting.

6. Listen to Your Body

One of the most important aspects of the Epi Diet is learning to listen to your body. Pay attention to how different foods affect your feelings. Notice when you're hungry and when you're full. Eating mindfully promotes a healthier relationship with food and can help you avoid overeating.

7. Embrace Variety

Eating various foods ensures that your body receives all the nutrients it needs. Experiment with various fruits, vegetables, grains, and proteins. Try new recipes and cuisines. Variety makes your daily meals more interesting and delightful.

8. Don't Be Too Hard on Yourself

It's important to remember that nobody is perfect. You might have days when you slip up or indulge in something not on the plan. That's okay. Don't beat yourself up over it. Recognize it, learn from it, and move forward. What matters most is getting back on track and continuing your journey.

9. Prepare for Cravings

Cravings are natural, especially when you're changing your eating habits. Prepare for them by having healthy snacks available. Nuts, seeds, fruit, and yogurt are great options. Sometimes, a small indulgence is okay too. A piece of dark chocolate can satisfy a sweet tooth without derailing your progress.

10. Cook at Home

Cooking at home allows you to control what ingredients go into your meals. It's a great way to ensure you're using fresh, whole ingredients. Plus, cooking can be a fun and relaxing activity. Get creative in the kitchen, try new recipes, and enjoy the process of making your meals.

11. Celebrate Small Wins

Recognize and celebrate your milestones, no matter how little they are. Did you choose a healthy snack instead of junk food? That's a win. Cooked a homemade meal instead of ordering takeout? Another win.

Celebrating these moments helps build a positive mindset and keeps you motivated.

12. Be Patient
Change takes time. Your body requires time to adapt to new dietary habits. Be patient with yourself and take your time to go through the process. You might not see immediate results, but with consistency, you will notice positive changes in your health and well-being.

13. Enjoy the Journey
The Epi Diet focuses on the journey rather than the destination. Enjoy discovering new foods, flavors, and recipes. Take pleasure in fueling your body with nutritious, delectable foods. Embrace the changes and find joy in the process of becoming healthier and happier.

3
Meal Planning and Preparation

Meal planning and preparation are like the roadmap and tools for your journey on the Epi Diet. They guide you, save you time, and make sure you always have healthy, delicious options at your fingertips. With a bit of planning and prep, you can transform your kitchen into a haven of nourishment and joy.

Imagine knowing exactly what you will eat for the entire week. No more last-minute scrambles or unhealthy takeout. That's the power of meal planning. Begin by setting aside time each week to arrange your meals. It doesn't have to be complicated. A simple outline of what you'll have for breakfast, lunch, dinner, and snacks is enough.

Meal planning is all about making your life easier and ensuring you stick to your healthy eating goals. I have provided a 14 days meal plan that will perfectly suit your weight loss journey.

Making a Grocery List

With your meal plan in hand, it's time to make a grocery list. Go through each recipe and write down the ingredients you need. Check your cupboard and refrigerator to determine what you already have. This step prevents you from buying unnecessary items and helps you stay within your budget.

A well-organized grocery list saves time at the store. Group items by category – produce, dairy, grains, etc. This way, you can easily find everything you need without backtracking. Shopping with a list also helps you stick to your healthy eating goals, reducing the temptation to buy unhealthy snacks.

Prepping Your Meals

Meal prep is a game-changer. It saves time, reduces stress, and ensures you always have healthy options ready to go. If you're just starting off with meal planning, start small. Choose one or two recipes to prepare in advance.

Begin by washing and chopping your fruits and vegetables. Keep them in airtight containers in the refrigerator. Pre-cook grains like quinoa or brown rice and portion them out for easy access. Cook your proteins – grilled chicken, baked tofu, or roasted chickpeas – and store them separately.

Batch cooking is another great strategy. Make a large batch of a recipe and divide it into individual portions. Soups, stews, casseroles, and grain bowls work well for batch cooking. Freeze some portions for later in the week or month.

Quick and Easy Meals

Life gets busy, and you might need a quick dinner. Having a few go-to recipes that are fast and easy can save the day. Think stir-fries, salads, and wraps. Keep ingredients for these meals on hand, so you can whip them up in no time.

For example, a stir-fry with mixed vegetables, tofu, and a simple sauce can be ready in minutes. A hearty salad with leafy greens, grilled chicken, nuts, and a homemade dressing is both nutritious and delicious. Wraps made with whole-grain tortillas, hummus, veggies, and lean protein are perfect for a quick, satisfying meal.

Navigating Your Kitchen

Your kitchen is the heart of your home, a place where nourishment and creativity come together. Navigating it with confidence and ease can transform the way you approach cooking and eating. It's where you'll prepare the meals that fuel your body and soul, making the journey on the Epi Diet both enjoyable and fulfilling. Let's dive into the essentials of mastering your kitchen.

1. Organizing Your Space
A well-organized kitchen is the first step to successful cooking. Start by decluttering your space. Remove any items you don't use regularly. Keep your countertops clear, so you have plenty of room to work. An organized kitchen makes it easier to find what you need and keeps the cooking process smooth and stress-free.

Arrange your utensils, pots, and pans within easy reach. Store your most-used items in accessible places. For example, keep your knives, cutting boards, and mixing bowls close to your prep area. Store frequently used spices and oils within arms reach or near the burner. This way, everything is at your fingertips when you need it.

2. Stocking Your Pantry
A well-stocked pantry is the backbone of a healthy kitchen. Fill it with staple ingredients that align with the Epi Diet. Whole grains like quinoa, brown rice, and oats provide the base for many meals. Chickpeas, lentils, and beans are good

sources of fiber and protein. Nuts, seeds, and dried fruits make for great snacks and additions to various dishes.

Keep a variety of spices and herbs on hand to add flavor and nutrition to your meals. Basic spices like salt, pepper, garlic powder, and cinnamon are essentials. Fresh herbs, such as basil, cilantro, and parsley, can add more flavor to any dish. Having these ingredients readily available makes meal preparation quicker and easier.

3. Setting Up Your Fridge

Your fridge should be a treasure trove of fresh, wholesome ingredients. Keep it organized and clean. Store fruits and vegetables in the crisper drawers to keep them fresh longer. Wash and chop veggies ahead of time and store them in clear containers, so they're ready to use. This prompts you to take more fresh produce.

Arrange your fridge so that healthier options are at eye level, making them the first thing you see when you open the door. Keep lean proteins like chicken, fish, and tofu on a separate shelf. Dairy or dairy alternatives should be easy to access. Leftovers should be stored in clear containers, labeled with the date, so you remember to use them.

4. Essential Kitchen Tools

Having the right tools increases both the fun and efficiency of cooking. Invest in quality items that will last. A good set of knives is crucial. A sharp chef's knife, a paring knife, and a serrated knife cover most of your needs. Cutting boards, preferably one for vegetables and another for meats, are essential for safe food prep.

Other must-haves include mixing bowls, measuring cups and spoons, a blender, a food processor, and non-stick cookware. Steamer baskets, salad spinners, and storage containers are also extremely useful. These tools make it easier to prepare a variety of healthy meals.

5. Creating a Prep Station

Designate a specific area in your kitchen as your prep station. This is where you'll do most of your chopping, mixing, and assembling. Keep it well-lit and free of clutter. Have your knives, cutting boards, and mixing bowls within arm's reach. This setup streamlines your cooking process and makes it more enjoyable.

6. Embracing Meal Prep

Meal prep can be a game-changer for busy weeks. Dedicate a day to preparing several meals in advance. Chop vegetables, cook grains, and proteins, and portion them into containers. This way, you have ready-to-eat meals all week. Meal prep saves time and reduces the temptation to order takeout.

Batch cooking is also effective. Prepare a large batch of soups, stews, or casseroles and freeze individual portions. This ensures you always have a healthy meal on hand, even on your busiest days. Just reheat and enjoy.

7. Making Cleanup Easy

A clean kitchen is a happy kitchen. Make cleanup part of your cooking routine. Clean as you go to avoid a huge mess at the end. Keep a trash can or compost bin nearby for easy disposal of food scraps. Wipe down surfaces regularly to prevent spills from becoming stains.

Invest in a good dish soap and scrubber. Soak pots and pans immediately after use to make cleaning easier. If you have a dishwasher, load it as you cook, so you're not left with a pile of dirty dishes. A tidy kitchen makes cooking more enjoyable and less stressful.

8. Enjoying the Process

Cooking should be a joyful experience. Play your favorite music or a podcast while you cook. Experiment with new recipes and ingredients. Engage your family and friends in the process. Cooking together may be an enjoyable and bonding hobby.

Take pride in the meals you create. Even if a dish doesn't turn out perfectly, celebrate the effort you put into making something healthy and delicious. The more you cook, the more confident you'll become, and the more you'll enjoy it.

9. Adapting to Your Needs

Your kitchen setup should work for you. If something isn't working, change it. Maybe you need more counter space or a better knife. Perhaps you prefer storing grains in glass jars instead of plastic containers. Adapt your kitchen to suit your cooking style and preferences. This flexibility ensures your kitchen remains a place of comfort and efficiency.

Substitutions and Alternatives

When embarking on a journey towards healthier eating, flexibility and adaptability are key. One of the most empowering aspects of the Epi Diet is the ability to make substitutions and find alternatives that work for you. Life is dynamic, and our diets should reflect that flexibility. Whether due to allergies, preferences, or simply the desire for variety, knowing how to substitute ingredients can make your culinary experience more enjoyable and accessible.

Embracing Substitutions:
Substitutions are more than just a practical necessity; they are an opportunity to explore new flavors and ingredients. Each substitution is a chance to expand your palate, try something new, and discover combinations you might not have considered before. This creative approach to cooking keeps meals exciting and enjoyable, making it easier to stick to your healthy eating goals.

Gluten-Free Alternatives:
For those who need to avoid gluten, there are many wonderful alternatives available. Instead of traditional wheat flour, you can use almond flour, coconut flour, or oat flour in your baking. These flours not only provide a different texture but also bring their unique flavors and nutritional benefits to your dishes. Quinoa, rice, and corn are excellent substitutes for wheat-based grains, offering a variety of tastes and textures.

Dairy-Free Options:

If dairy is not suitable for you, there are numerous dairy-free alternatives that are just as delicious and nutritious. Almond milk, coconut milk, and oat milk can easily replace cow's milk in most recipes. Coconut yogurt and cashew cream are great substitutes for dairy for people who miss the creamy texture of dairy products. Nutritional yeast can be used to mimic the cheesy flavor in vegan dishes, adding a savory note to your meals without the dairy.

Plant-Based Proteins:

For those who choose to follow a plant-based diet or want to incorporate more plant-based meals, there are plenty of protein-rich options available. Beans, lentils, tofu, and tempeh are excellent sources of protein that can easily replace meat in many dishes. These ingredients are versatile and can be seasoned to match any flavor profile, making them a great addition to your culinary repertoire.

Healthy Fat Swaps:

Healthy fats are vital for our health but are not all the same. Substituting unhealthy fats with healthier options can make a significant difference. Instead of butter, try using avocado, olive oil, or coconut oil in your cooking. These fats not only provide essential nutrients but also add rich, delicious flavors to your dishes. Avocado can also be used as a creamy substitute in desserts and smoothies, offering a nutritious twist.

Sugar Alternatives:

Reducing sugar intake is a common goal for many on the Epi Diet. Fortunately, there are plenty of natural sweeteners that can be used in place of refined sugar. Honey, maple syrup, and agave nectar are wonderful options that add sweetness without the negative effects of processed sugar. For those looking for a low-calorie alternative, stevia and monk fruit sweeteners are excellent choices that don't compromise on taste.

Egg Substitutes:

Whether you're allergic to eggs or following a vegan diet, there are several effective substitutes for eggs in baking and cooking. Flaxseed meal and chia seeds can be mixed with water to create a gel-like consistency that works well as a binder. Applesauce and mashed bananas are also great alternatives, adding moisture and sweetness to your baked goods. Silken tofu can replace eggs in savory dishes like quiches and scrambles, providing a similar texture and protein content.

Flavor Enhancers:

Herbs and spices are the unsung heroes of healthy cooking. They allow you to enhance flavors without relying on salt or unhealthy additives. Try out several combinations until you identify which ones work best for you. Fresh herbs like basil, cilantro, and parsley can enhance any dish, while spices like cumin, paprika, and turmeric offer depth and complexity. Vinegars and citrus juices are also excellent for adding acidity and balancing flavors.

Whole Grains and Legumes:

Replacing refined grains with whole grains is an easy and effective approach to increase the nutritional value of your

40

meals. Brown rice, quinoa, farro, and barley are excellent alternatives to white rice and pasta. These grains provide more fiber, vitamins, and minerals, helping you stay full and energized. Legumes, such as chickpeas, black beans, and lentils, are versatile and nutrient-dense, making them a great substitute for meat in many recipes.

Nut and Seed Butters:

Nut and seed butters are fantastic sources of healthy fats and proteins. If you have a peanut allergy or simply want to try something new, there are plenty of alternatives to peanut butter. Almond butter, cashew butter, sunflower seed butter, and tahini are all delicious options that can be used in smoothies, baked goods, and savory dishes. Each brings its unique flavor and nutritional profile, offering endless possibilities.

Creative Vegetable Substitutes:

Many classic recipes may be made with vegetables as low-carb substitutes. Cauliflower rice and zucchini noodles are popular substitutes for rice and pasta, offering a lighter and more nutrient-dense option. Portobello mushrooms can replace burger patties or serve as a base for pizzas. Sweet potatoes can be spiralized into noodles or used in place of regular potatoes for a healthier twist.

14 Days Meal Plan

Day 1
Breakfast: Energizing Smoothie Bowls
Lunch: Grilled Chicken and Quinoa Salad
Dinner: Baked Salmon with

Asparagus	Almond Butter
Day 2	**Lunch:** Chickpea and Avocado Salad
Breakfast: Avocado and Egg Toast	**Dinner:** Quinoa and Veggie Stuffed Acorn Squash
Lunch: Chickpea and Veggie Stew	**Day 7**
Dinner: Zucchini Noodles with Pesto	**Breakfast:** Sweet Potato Breakfast Hash
Day 3	**Lunch:** Spinach and Feta Stuffed Peppers
Breakfast: Berry and Nut Overnight Oats	**Dinner:** Turkey Meatballs with Spaghetti Squash
Lunch: Turkey and Avocado Wrap	**Day 8**
Dinner: Chicken and Broccoli Stir-Fry	**Breakfast:** Breakfast Tacos
Day 4	**Lunch:** Veggie Sushi Rolls
Breakfast: Veggie Frittata	**Dinner:** Eggplant Parmesan
Lunch: Greek Salad with Tofu	**Day 9**
Dinner: Creamy Garlic Chicken Breast	**Breakfast:** Whole Grain Pancakes with Fresh Fruit
Day 5	**Lunch:** Tuna and White Bean Salad
Breakfast: Spinach and Mushroom Omelet	**Dinner:** Shrimp and Vegetable Skewers
Lunch: Cauliflower Rice Stir-Fry	**Day 10**
Dinner: Black Bean and Sweet Potato Tacos	**Breakfast:** Veggie-Packed Breakfast Burrito
Day 6	
Breakfast: Berry Oatmeal with	

Lunch: Tomato Basil Soup with Grilled Cheese
Dinner: Melt In Your Mouth (MIYM) Chicken Breasts
Day 11
Breakfast: Energizing Smoothie Bowls
Lunch: Grilled Chicken and Quinoa Salad
Dinner: Baked Salmon with Asparagus
Day 12
Breakfast: Avocado and Egg Toast
Lunch: Chickpea and Veggie Stew
Dinner: Zucchini Noodles with Pesto
Day 13
Breakfast: Berry and Nut Overnight Oats
Lunch: Turkey and Avocado Wrap
Dinner: Chicken and Broccoli Stir-Fry
Day 14
Breakfast: Veggie Frittata
Lunch: Greek Salad with Tofu

Dinner: Creamy Garlic Chicken Breast

The beauty of the Epi Diet is its adaptability. It's about making choices that fit your lifestyle and preferences while nourishing your body. By embracing substitutions and alternatives, you are not only making healthier choices but also enriching your culinary experience. By celebrating health and taste at every meal, this mindful eating style keeps you in touch with your food.

Don't be afraid to experiment in the kitchen. Trying new ingredients and recipes can be a fun and rewarding experience. Use this journey as an opportunity to discover what works best for you. Let your taste buds guide you and enjoy the process of creating meals that are both delicious and nutritious.

Understanding the reasons behind substitutions and how they benefit your health empowers you to make informed decisions. Knowledge is a powerful tool in maintaining a healthy diet. By knowing which ingredients to swap and why, you can confidently create meals that support your well-being.

The journey of maintaining the Epi Diet is an ongoing adventure filled with learning and growth. Embracing substitutions and alternatives is a key part of this journey, allowing you to adapt to your unique needs and preferences while staying true to your health goals.

4
Breakfast Bliss

Energizing Smoothie Bowls

> **Prep Time:** 10 minutes
> **Cook Time:** Not required
> **Serving:** 1 bowl

Ingredients:

For the Smoothie Base:

- 1 ripe banana, frozen
- 1/2 cup frozen berries (such as blueberries, strawberries, or raspberries)
- 1/2 cup spinach or kale
- 1/2 cup unsweetened almond milk
- 1 tablespoon chia seeds
- 1 tablespoon almond butter

For the Toppings:

- Fresh berries (blueberries, strawberries, raspberries)
- Sliced banana
- Granola and Chia seeds
- Coconut flakes
- Nuts (almonds, walnuts, or pecans)
- Honey or maple syrup (optional)

Procedures:

1) Freeze the banana and berries the night before to ensure your smoothie bowl is thick and creamy.
2) Gather all the ingredients and set up your blender.
3) In a high-speed blender, combine the frozen banana, frozen berries, spinach or kale (if using), almond milk, chia seeds, and almond butter.
4) Blend until smooth and creamy. To make sure everything is properly blended, you might need to pause and scrape along the sides of the blender.

5) If the mixture is too thick, add a little more almond milk, one tablespoon at a time, until you reach the desired consistency.

6) Pour the smoothie into a bowl. Arrange your toppings artfully on top of the smoothie. You can create sections with each topping or mix them all together. Make it visually appealing.

7) Enjoy your smoothie bowl right away while it's still cold and fresh.

Nutritional Value:

Calories: 400; Protein: 10g; Fat: 20g; Carbs: 55g; Fiber: 12g

Avocado and Egg Toast

➢ **Prep Time:** 5mins
➢ **Cook Time:** 10mins
➢ **Servings:** 1

Ingredients:

- 1 ripe avocado
- 1 large egg
- One piece of sourdough or whole-grain bread
- Salt and pepper to taste
- Red pepper flakes (optional)
- Lemon juice (optional)
- Cherry tomatoes, halved
- Fresh herbs (parsley, cilantro, or chives)
- Feta cheese, crumbled

Procedures:

1) Slice the avocado in half, remove the pit, and scoop the flesh into a bowl.

2) Toast the slice of bread until it's golden and crisp.

3) **Fried:** Heat a small non-stick skillet over medium heat. Add a little oil or butter, then crack the egg into the skillet. Cook until the whites are set and the yolk reaches your desired doneness (sunny-side up or over-easy).

4) **Poached:** Boil a pot of water. Pour a little vinegar into the water. After cracking the egg into a small bowl, carefully place it in the water that is simmering. Cook for 3-4 minutes until the whites are set but the yolk is still runny. Remove with a slotted spoon.

5) **Scrambled:** Crack the egg into a bowl, whisk it with a little salt and pepper, then cook in a non-stick skillet over medium heat, stirring constantly until the eggs are soft and fluffy.

6) While the egg is cooking, mash the avocado in the bowl until smooth. Add a pinch of salt, pepper, and a squeeze of lemon juice (if using) to taste.

7) Spread the mashed avocado evenly over the toasted bread.

8) Place the cooked egg on top of the avocado. Sprinkle red pepper flakes for a bit of heat. Add cherry tomatoes, fresh herbs, or crumbled feta cheese for extra flavor and texture.

Nutritional Value:

Calories: 350; Protein: 12g; Fat: 25g; Carbs: 25g; Fiber: 10g

Berry and Nut Overnight Oats

➤ **Prep Time:** 10mins
➤ **Cook Time:** Not required
➤ **Servings:** 1

Ingredients:

- 1/2 cup rolled oats
- 1/2 cup unsweetened almond milk
- 1/4 cup Greek yogurt
- 1 tablespoon chia seeds
- 1/2 teaspoon vanilla extract
- 1 tablespoon honey
- 1/2 cup mixed: strawberries, blueberries, raspberries
- 2 tsp finely chopped nuts (pecans, walnuts, or almonds)
- 1 tablespoon flaxseeds

Procedures:

1) The rolled oats, almond milk, Greek yogurt (if used), chia seeds, vanilla extract, honey, or maple syrup should all be combined in a mason jar or small bowl. Make sure all components are fully combined by stirring well.

2) Gently fold in the mixed berries. You can use fresh or frozen berries depending on what you have on hand. The berries will add a burst of flavor and a beautiful color to your oats.

3) Sprinkle the chopped nuts and flaxseeds (if using) on top of the mixture. The nuts add a delightful crunch and extra protein, while the flaxseeds boost the nutritional value.

4) Cover the jar or bowl with a lid or plastic wrap and refrigerate overnight. This allows the oats to absorb the liquid and soften,

and the flavors to meld together.

5) Stir well the oats in the morning. Add a small amount of almond milk if the mixture is too thick to get the right consistency. Enjoy your overnight oats straight from the jar or transfer them to a bowl.

Nutritional Value:

Calories: 400 kal; Protein: 15g;

Fat: 20g; Carbs: 50g; Fiber: 12g

Veggie Frittata

➤ **Prep Time:** 15mins
➤ **Cook Time:** 25mins
➤ **Servings:** 4

Ingredients:

- 8 large eggs
- 1/4 cup milk (dairy or non-dairy)
- 1/2 cup shredded cheese; cheddar, feta, or mozzarella
- 1 tablespoon olive oil
- 1 small onion, diced
- 1 bell pepper, diced
- 1 zucchini, sliced
- 1 cup cherry tomatoes, halved
- 1 cup spinach leaves
- 2 cloves garlic, minced
- Salt and pepper to taste
- Fresh herbs like parsley, basil, or chives as garnish.

Procedures:

1) Preheat your oven to 375°F (190°C).

2) In an oven safe skillet, heat the olive oil over medium heat. Add the diced onion and bell pepper, and sauté until they begin to soften, about 3-4 minutes.

3) Add the zucchini slices and cherry tomatoes to the skillet. Cook until the veggies are soft, about 3 to 4 more minutes.

4) Add the spinach and minced garlic, stirring until the spinach is wilted. To taste, add salt and pepper to the veggies.

5) In a large bowl, whisk together the eggs and milk until well combined. If using cheese, combine it with the egg mixture.

6) Pour the egg mixture over the sautéed vegetables in the skillet. Use a spatula to gently stir and evenly distribute the vegetables and eggs.

7) Cook on the stovetop over medium heat for about 5 minutes, until the edges begin to set but the center is still slightly runny.

8) Transfer the skillet to the preheated oven. Bake for 15-20 minutes, or until the frittata is fully set and golden brown on top. You can check doneness by inserting a toothpick into the center; if it comes out clean, the frittata is ready.

9) After taking the pan out of the oven, give the frittata some time to cool. Serve warm, sliced into wedges, and garnish with fresh herbs.

Nutritional Value:

Calories: 250; Protein: 18g; Fat: 15g; Carbs: 10g; Fiber: 3g

Spinach and Mushroom Omelet

➤ **Prep Time:** 10mins
➤ **Cook Time:** 10mins
➤ **Servings:** 1

Ingredients:

- 3 large eggs
- 1/4 cup milk (dairy or non-dairy)

- 1 tablespoon olive oil or butter
- 1/2 cup fresh spinach leaves, chopped
- 1/2 cup mushrooms, sliced (button, cremini, or shiitake)
- 1/4 cup shredded cheese (cheddar, Swiss, or feta)
- Salt and pepper to taste
- Fresh herbs (such as chives or parsley) for garnish

Procedures:

1) Heat the olive oil or butter in a nonstick pan over medium heat. Sauté the sliced mushrooms for 3-4 minutes until they begin to hue and release moisture.

2) Add the chopped spinach to the skillet and cook for another 1-2 minutes until the spinach is wilted. Add a dash of pepper and salt for seasoning. Remove the veggies from the skillet and put them aside.

3) In a medium bowl, whisk together the eggs and milk until well combined. Add a pinch of pepper and salt for seasoning.

4) Wipe the skillet clean and heat it over medium-low heat. Add a small amount of olive oil or butter to coat the pan.

5) Pour the egg mixture into the skillet, swirling it to cover the bottom evenly. Cook uncovered, for two to three minutes, or until the center is still a little runny and the edges begin to harden.

6) Sprinkle the sautéed mushrooms and spinach evenly over one half of the omelet. If using cheese, add it on top of the vegetables.

7) Using a spatula, gently fold the other half of the omelet over the filling. Press down lightly to seal.

8) Continue to cook for another 1-2 minutes until the cheese is melted and the eggs are fully set but still tender.

9) Slide the omelet onto a plate and garnish with fresh herbs if desired. Serve immediately.

Nutritional Value:

Calories: 350; Protein: 22g; Fat: 25g; Carbs: 7g; Fiber: 2g

Berry Oatmeal with Almond Butter

- ➤ **Prep Time:** 5mins
- ➤ **Cook Time:** 10mins
- ➤ **Servings:** 1

Ingredients:

- 1/2 cup rolled oats
- One cup of unsweetened almond milk or water
- Half a cup of mixed raspberries, blueberries, and strawberries, either frozen or fresh
- 1 tablespoon almond butter
- One tablespoon of maple syrup or honey (optional)
- 1/2 teaspoon vanilla extract
- 1/4 teaspoon cinnamon (optional)
- A pinch of salt
- Toppings (optional): additional fresh berries, sliced banana, chia seeds, nuts, shredded coconut

Procedures:

1) In a small saucepan, combine the rolled oats, water or almond milk, and a pinch of salt. Allow it to a boil on medium-high heat. After that, lower the heat to a simmer and cook, stirring periodically, for about five minutes.

2) Stir in the vanilla extract and cinnamon (if using). Continue to cook for another 2-3 minutes until the oats are creamy and

have absorbed most of the liquid.

3) Add the mixed berries to the oatmeal. If using fresh berries, gently fold them in. If using frozen berries, let them cook with the oats for an additional 2 minutes until they are heated through and slightly softened.

4) Remove the saucepan from the heat and stir in the almond butter until it is fully incorporated and the oatmeal is creamy.

5) If you prefer a sweeter oatmeal, drizzle with honey or maple syrup and stir to combine.

6) Pour the oatmeal into a bowl. Top with additional fresh berries, sliced banana, chia seeds, nuts, or shredded coconut as desired. Serve warm and enjoy.

Nutritional Value:

Calories: 400 kal; Protein: 10g;

Fat: 20g; Carbs: 50g

Sweet Potato Breakfast Hash

➤ **Prep Time:** 10mins
➤ **Cook Time:** 30mins
➤ **Servings:** 4

Ingredients:

- 2 big sweet potatoes, skinned and chopped
- 1 red bell pepper, diced
- 1 green bell pepper, diced
- 1 small red onion, diced
- 2 cloves garlic, minced
- 1 tablespoon olive oil
- 1 teaspoon smoked paprika
- 1/2 teaspoon ground cumin
- 1/2 teaspoon chili powder
- Salt and pepper to taste
- 4 large eggs (optional)

- fresh cilantro or parsley (optional)

Procedures:

1) Peel and dice the sweet potatoes into small, evenly-sized cubes.

2) Dice the red and green bell peppers and the red onion. Mince the garlic cloves.

3) In a big skillet, warm the olive oil over medium heat. When the sweet potatoes start to soften and become golden brown, add the diced sweet potatoes and simmer, turning periodically, for about ten minutes.

4) Add the diced bell peppers and red onion to the skillet. Continue to cook for another 5-7 minutes, stirring occasionally, until the vegetables are tender and the onions are translucent.

5) Stir in the minced garlic, smoked paprika, ground cumin, chili powder, salt, and pepper. Cook for another 2-3 minutes, allowing the spices to blend and the garlic to become fragrant.

6) If you want to add eggs, make four small wells in the hash mixture. Crack an egg into each well. Cover the skillet and heat for 5-7 minutes, or until the eggs reach your desired doneness. For runny yolks, cook for a shorter time; for firm yolks, cook longer.

7) Remove the skillet from the heat. You can garnish with fresh parsley or cilantro, if you want. Serve hot, directly from the skillet or transfer to individual plates.

Nutritional Value:

Calories: 300; Protein: 12g; Fat: 12g; Carbs: 30g; Fiber: 7g

Breakfast Tacos

➤ **Prep Time:** 10mins
➤ **Cook Time:** 10mins
➤ **Servings:** 4

Ingredients:

- 8 small corn or whole-wheat tortillas
- 6 large eggs
- 1/4 cup milk (dairy or non-dairy)
- 1 tablespoon olive oil or butter
- 1 small red bell pepper, diced
- 1 small green bell pepper, diced
- 1 small red onion, diced
- One cup of rinsed and drained black beans
- 1/2 cup shredded cheese (cheddar or Monterey Jack)
- 1 avocado, sliced
- 1/4 cup fresh salsa
- Fresh cilantro, chopped
- Salt and pepper to taste
- Hot sauce (optional)

Procedures:

1) Heat olive oil or butter in a skillet over medium heat, sauté diced bell peppers and red onion until tender. Add black beans, cook until heated through, season with salt and pepper. Set aside.

2) Whisk eggs and milk in a bowl, season with salt and pepper. Clean skillet, add oil or butter, and cook eggs, stirring gently until scrambled and just set.

3) Heat the tortillas over a gas flame or in a dry skillet until they are flexible.

4) Divide scrambled eggs among tortillas, top with sautéed vegetables and black beans.

5) Sprinkle with shredded cheese, add avocado slices, spoon fresh salsa, and garnish with chopped

cilantro. Optionally, add hot sauce.

6) Serve warm with additional salsa and hot sauce on the side. Enjoy!

Nutritional Value:

Calories: 400; Protein: 22g; Fat: 25g; Carbs: 35g; Fiber: 10g

Whole Grain Pancakes with Fresh Fruit

- ➤ **Prep Time:** 10mins
- ➤ **Cook Time:** 20mins
- ➤ **Servings:** 4

Ingredients:

- 1 cup whole wheat flour
- 1/2 cup rolled oats
- 2 tablespoons flaxseed meal (optional)
- 2 tablespoons brown sugar or honey
- 1 tablespoon baking powder
- 1/2 teaspoon baking soda
- 1/2 teaspoon salt
- 1 teaspoon cinnamon (optional)
- 1 + 1/4 cups milk (dairy or non-dairy)
- 1 large egg
- Two tablespoons of melted butter or coconut oil
- 1 teaspoon vanilla extract
- Fresh fruit for topping (such as berries, banana slices, or peach slices)
- For serving; honey or maple syrup (optional).
- Additional toppings (optional): Greek yogurt, nuts, seeds

Procedures:

1) Combine whole wheat flour, rolled oats, flaxseed meal (if using), brown sugar or honey, baking powder, baking soda,

salt, and cinnamon in a large bowl.

2) In a separate bowl, whisk together milk, egg, melted coconut oil or butter, and vanilla extract.

3) Pour wet ingredients into dry ingredients and stir gently until just combined, leaving a few lumps.

4) Preheat a non-stick skillet or griddle over medium heat and lightly grease with coconut oil or butter.

5) Pour 1/4 cup of batter onto the skillet for each pancake, cook until bubbles form and edges set (2-3 minutes), flip and cook until golden brown (2-3 minutes).

6) Transfer cooked pancakes to a plate and keep warm. Repeat with remaining batter.

7) Stack pancakes on plates, top with fresh fruit, drizzle with maple syrup or honey, and add additional toppings like Greek yogurt, nuts, or seeds if desired. Enjoy!

Nutritional Value:

Calories: 350; Protein: 10g; Fat: 12g; Carbs: 50g; Fiber: 8g

Veggie-Packed Breakfast Burrito

➢ **Prep Time:** 10mins
➢ **Cook Time:** 20mins
➢ **Servings:** 4

Ingredients:

- 4 large whole-grain tortillas
- 6 large eggs
- 1/4 cup milk (dairy or non-dairy)
- 1 tablespoon olive oil or butter

- 1 small red onion, diced
- 1 red bell pepper, diced
- 1 green bell pepper, diced
- 1 cup mushrooms, sliced
- 1 cup spinach, chopped
- One cup of rinsed and drained black beans
- 1/2 cup shredded cheese (cheddar or Monterey Jack)
- Salt and pepper to taste
- 1 avocado, sliced (optional)
- Fresh salsa or pico de gallo (optional)
- Fresh cilantro for garnish (optional)
- Hot sauce (optional)

Procedures:

1) Heat olive oil or butter in a skillet over medium heat, add diced red onion, and sauté until it begins to soften.
2) Add the mushrooms, red and green bell peppers, and simmer until the mushrooms release moisture and become soft. Add spinach and cook until wilted. Add salt and pepper for seasoning and set it aside.
3) Whisk your eggs and milk and sprinkle salt and pepper.
4) Wipe skillet, add more oil or butter if needed, pour in egg mixture, and cook gently until scrambled and just set. Add black beans and stir to combine, then remove from heat.
5) Lay a tortilla flat, spoon a quarter of the vegetable mixture and scrambled eggs onto the center, sprinkle with cheese if using. Fold sides over filling and roll up from the bottom.
6) Serve warm, topped with avocado, salsa or pico de gallo, and fresh cilantro. Add hot sauce for extra spice. Enjoy!

Nutritional Value:

Calories:400; Protein:22g; Fat:20g; Carbs:40g

5
Lunch Recipes

Grilled Chicken and Quinoa Salad

➢ **Prep Time:** 15mins
➢ **Cook Time:** 25mins
➢ **Servings:** 4

Ingredients:

For the Salad:

- 1 cup quinoa, rinsed
- 2 cups water or chicken broth
- 2 large chicken breasts
- 1 tablespoon olive oil
- Salt and pepper to taste
- 1 teaspoon garlic powder
- 1 teaspoon paprika
- 1 cucumber, diced
- 1 cup cherry tomatoes, halved
- 1 red bell pepper, diced
- 1/2 red onion, finely chopped
- 1 avocado, diced
- 1/4 cup crumbled feta cheese
- Fresh parsley or cilantro

For the Dressing:

- 1/4 cup olive oil
- 2 tablespoons lemon juice
- 1 tablespoon red wine vinegar
- 1 teaspoon Dijon mustard
- 1 clove garlic, minced
- Salt and pepper to taste

Procedures:

1) Boil water or chicken broth in a saucepan, add rinsed quinoa, reduce heat, cover, and simmer until tender. Use a fork to fluff it and set aside to cool.

2) Set the grill pan or grill to medium-high heat.

3) Rub chicken breasts with olive oil, season with salt, pepper, garlic powder, and paprika.

4) Grill chicken for 6-7 minutes per side until fully cooked. Let rest, then slice into thin strips.

5) Combine diced cucumber, cherry tomatoes, red bell

pepper, red onion, and avocado in a large mixing bowl.

6) Whisk together olive oil, lemon juice, red wine vinegar, Dijon mustard, minced garlic, salt, and pepper in a small bowl or jar.

7) Add cooked quinoa and grilled chicken strips to the vegetables, pour dressing over, and toss gently.

8) Sprinkle with crumbled feta cheese (if using) and garnish with chopped parsley or cilantro. After dividing among four bowls or plates, serve right away.

Nutritional Value:

Calories: 500; Protein: 32g; Fat: 25g; Carbs: 35g; Fiber: 8g

Chickpea and Veggie Stew

➤ **Prep Time:** 15mins
➤ **Cook Time:** 35mins
➤ **Servings:** 4

Ingredients:

- 2 tablespoons olive oil
- 1 large onion, diced
- 3 cloves garlic, minced
- 2 carrots, peeled and diced
- 2 celery stalks, diced
- 1 red bell pepper, diced
- 1 zucchini, diced
- One big sweet potato, skinned and chopped
- 1 can (15 ounces) chickpeas
- 1 can (14.5 ounces) tomatoes
- 4 cups vegetable broth

- 1 teaspoon ground cumin
- 1 teaspoon ground coriander
- 1 teaspoon smoked paprika
- 1/2 teaspoon ground turmeric
- 1/2 teaspoon ground cinnamon
- Salt and pepper to taste
- 1 cup kale or spinach, chopped
- Juice of 1 lemon
- Fresh parsley or cilantro for garnish

Procedures:

1) Dice onion, carrots, celery, red bell pepper, zucchini, and sweet potato. Mince garlic.
2) Heat olive oil in a large pot over medium heat, add diced onion, and cook until softened.
3) Add minced garlic, carrots, and celery; cook until beginning to soften. Add red bell pepper, zucchini, and sweet potato; cook further.
4) Stir in ground cumin, coriander, smoked paprika, turmeric, cinnamon, salt, and pepper to coat vegetables.
5) Add chickpeas, diced tomatoes, and vegetable broth, stirring to combine.
6) Bring to a boil, then reduce heat and simmer until vegetables are tender.
7) Stir in chopped kale or spinach and cook until wilted.
8) Stir in lemon juice, taste and adjust seasoning.
9) Ladle into bowls, garnish with fresh parsley or cilantro, and serve hot with crusty bread, rice, or quinoa if desired.

Nutritional Value:

Calories: 300kcal; Protein: 10g;

Fat: 10g; Carbs: 45g; Fiber: 12g

Turkey and Avocado Wrap

➤ **Prep Time:** 10mins
➤ **Cook Time:** No cooking
➤ **Servings:** 2

Ingredients:

- 2 large whole-grain tortillas
- 1 ripe avocado
- 1 tablespoon lemon juice
- Salt and pepper to taste
- 4 Deli-style turkey breast slices
- 1 cup of mixed greens, like lettuce, spinach, or arugula
- 1/2 cup cherry tomatoes, halved
- 1/4 cup red onion, thinly sliced
- 1/4 cup shredded carrots
- 1/4 cup of sliced red bell pepper
- 2 tablespoons hummus or Greek yogurt (optional)

Procedures:

1) Cut avocado in half, remove pit, scoop flesh into a bowl, mash until smooth, and stir in lemon juice. Season with salt and pepper.
2) Wash mixed greens, halve cherry tomatoes, thinly slice red onion and red bell pepper, and shred carrots.
3) Lay a tortilla flat, spread half the avocado mixture, add two slices of turkey, layer half the mixed greens, cherry tomatoes, red onion, shredded carrots, and red bell pepper. Optionally, spread hummus or Greek yogurt on top.
4) Fold sides of the tortilla over the filling, roll from the bottom to form a wrap. Repeat with remaining ingredients.
5) Serve each wrap right away after cutting it in half diagonally.

Nutritional Value:

Calories: 400 kcal; Protein: 22g;

Fat: 25g; Carbs: 35g; Fiber: 10g

Greek Salad with Tofu

➢ **Prep Time:** 15mins
➢ **Cook Time:** 15mins
➢ **Servings:** 4

Ingredients:

For the Salad:
- 1 block (14oz) extra-firm tofu
- 1 tablespoon olive oil
- 1 teaspoon dried oregano
- Salt and pepper to taste
- 4 cups romaine lettuce, chopped
- 1 large cucumber, diced
- 1 pint cherry tomatoes, halved
- 1 red bell pepper, diced
- 1/2 red onion, thinly sliced
- 1/2 cup Kalamata olives, pitted
- 1/2 cup feta cheese, crumbled
- Fresh parsley or dill for garnish

For the Dressing:
- 1/4 cup olive oil
- 2 tablespoons red wine vinegar
- 1 tablespoon lemon juice
- 1 teaspoon dried oregano
- 1 clove garlic, minced
- Salt and pepper to taste

Procedures:

1) Drain and press tofu to remove moisture, then cut into 1-inch cubes.

2) Heat olive oil in a skillet over medium heat, cook tofu with dried oregano, salt, and pepper until golden brown on all sides. Set aside.

3) Chop romaine lettuce, dice cucumber and red bell pepper, halve cherry tomatoes and Kalamata olives, and thinly slice red onion.

4) Whisk together olive oil, red wine vinegar, lemon juice, dried

oregano, minced garlic, salt, and pepper.

5) In a large bowl, combine romaine lettuce, cucumber, cherry tomatoes, red bell pepper, red onion, and Kalamata olives. Add cooked tofu cubes.

6) Pour dressing over the salad and toss gently to coat evenly.

7) Divide salad among plates or bowls, top with crumbled feta cheese if using, and garnish with fresh parsley or dill. Serve immediately. Enjoy!

Nutritional Value:

Calories: 400 kcal; Protein: 18g;

Fat: 30g; Carbs: 20g; Fiber: 7g

Cauliflower Rice Stir-Fry

➢ **Prep Time:** 15mins
➢ **Cook Time:** 15mins
➢ **Servings:** 4

Ingredients:

- 1 large head of cauliflower
- 2 tablespoons olive or sesame oil
- 1 medium onion, diced
- 2 cloves garlic, minced
- 1 tablespoon ginger, minced
- 1 red bell pepper, diced
- 1 yellow bell pepper, diced
- One cup of snow peas or snap peas
- 1 cup carrots, julienned
- 1 cup broccoli florets
- 1 cup mushrooms, sliced

- 3 green onions, sliced
- 3 tablespoons of tamari or soy sauce (gluten-free)
- 1 tablespoon rice vinegar
- 1 tablespoon sesame seeds
- Fresh cilantro for garnish
- Protein of choice (like tofu, chicken, or shrimp)

Procedures:

1) Remove leaves and core, cut into florets, and process into rice-sized pieces. Set aside.
2) Dice onion, mince garlic and ginger, chop bell peppers, snap peas, carrots, broccoli, and mushrooms. Slice green onions, keeping the white and green sections separate.
3) Cook tofu, chicken, or shrimp in a skillet until fully cooked. Set aside.
4) Heat oil in the skillet, sauté diced onion, then add garlic, ginger, and white parts of green onions. Cook until fragrant.
5) Add bell peppers, snap peas, carrots, broccoli, and mushrooms. Stir-fry until tender but crisp.
6) Push vegetables aside, add cauliflower rice, and cook until tender.
7) Stir in soy sauce or tamari and rice vinegar, cooking to coat evenly. Add cooked protein back into the skillet if using, mix to heat through.
8) Remove from heat, sprinkle with sesame seeds and green onions, and garnish with fresh cilantro if desired. Serve immediately. Enjoy!

Nutritional Value:

Calories: 200 kcal; Protein: 5g; Fat: 9g; Carbs: 20g; Fiber: 7g

Chickpea and Avocado Salad

- ➤ **Prep Time:** 15mins
- ➤ **Cook Time:** No Cooking
- ➤ **Servings:** 4

Ingredients:

- 1 can (15 ounces) chickpeas
- 2 ripe avocados, diced
- 1 cup cherry tomatoes, halved
- 1 small red onion, chopped
- 1 cucumber, diced
- 1 red bell pepper, diced
- 1/4 cup fresh cilantro or parsley
- 1/4 cup crumbled feta cheese
- 1/4 cup extra-virgin olive oil
- 2 tablespoons lemon juice
- 1 tablespoon red wine vinegar
- 1 clove garlic, minced
- Salt and pepper to taste

Procedures:

1) Drain and rinse chickpeas, place in a large mixing bowl.
2) Dice avocados, halve cherry tomatoes, finely chop red onion, dice cucumber and red bell pepper, chop fresh cilantro or parsley.
3) Whisk together olive oil, lemon juice, red wine vinegar, minced garlic, salt, and pepper in a small bowl.
4) Add diced avocado, cherry tomatoes, red onion, cucumber, red bell pepper, and chopped cilantro or parsley to the chickpeas.
5) Pour dressing over the salad, toss gently to coat evenly.
6) Sprinkle with crumbled feta cheese and gently toss.
7) Divide among plates or bowls and serve immediately. Enjoy!

Nutritional Value:

Calories: 400 kcal; Protein: 10g; Fat: 30g; Carbs: 30g; Fiber: 12g

Spinach and Feta Stuffed Peppers

➤ **Prep Time:** 20mins
➤ **Cook Time:** 40mins
➤ **Servings:** 4

Ingredients:

- 4 large bell peppers (any color)
- 1 tablespoon olive oil
- 1 small onion, chopped
- 2 cloves garlic, minced
- 6 cups fresh spinach, chopped
- One cup of brown rice or quinoa
- 1/2 cup crumbled feta cheese
- 1/4 cup sun-dried tomatoes, chopped (optional)
- 1/4 cup pine nuts, toasted (optional)
- 1 teaspoon dried oregano
- Salt and pepper to taste
- Fresh parsley for garnish

Procedures:

1) Set the oven to 375°F (190°C). Cut bell peppers in half, remove the seeds, and lay cut side up in a baking dish.

2) Heat olive oil in a skillet, cook chopped onion until softened, then add minced garlic and cook until fragrant. Add spinach and cook until wilted.

3) Combine cooked quinoa or brown rice, spinach mixture, crumbled feta cheese, sun-dried tomatoes (optional), toasted pine nuts (optional), dried oregano, salt, and pepper in a large bowl.

4) Spoon filling into bell pepper halves, pressing down lightly.

5) Cover baking dish with foil and bake for 25 minutes.

6) Remove foil and bake for an additional 10-15 minutes until peppers are tender.

7) Let stuffed peppers cool, garnish with fresh parsley if desired. Serve warm. Enjoy!

Nutritional Value:

Calories: 300 kcal; Protein: 10g; Fat: 15g; Carbs: 30g;; Fiber: 8g

Veggie Sushi Rolls

➤ **Prep Time:** 30mins
➤ **Cook Time:** 20mins
➤ **Servings:** 8 Rolls

Ingredients:

For the Sushi Rice:

- 2 cups sushi or short-grain rice
- 2 + 1/2 cups water
- 1/4 cup rice vinegar
- 2 tablespoons sugar
- 1 teaspoon salt

For the Rolls:

- 8 sheets of nori (seaweed)
- 1 cucumber, julienned
- 1 large carrot, julienned
- 1 avocado, thinly sliced
- 1 red bell pepper, julienned
- 1/2 cup sprouts (optional)
- 1/2 cup thinly sliced radishes (optional)

For Serving: Soy sauce or tamari (for gluten-free) or Pickled ginger or Wasabi or Sesame seeds

Procedures:

1) Place the rice in a fine-mesh strainer and rinse with cold water until clear.
2) Combine rinsed rice and 2 1/2 cups of water in a rice cooker or saucepan. Cover and boil the rice until it is cooked and the water is absorbed, then reduce the heat to simmer.
3) Mix rice vinegar, sugar, and salt in a small bowl until dissolved.
4) Transfer cooked rice to a bowl, pour vinegar mixture over, and gently fold in. Let cool to room temperature.

5) Cut the cucumber, carrot, and red bell pepper into matchsticks. Thinly slice avocado and radishes.

6) Place bamboo mat on a surface and cover with plastic wrap.

7) Lay nori sheet on the mat, wet fingers, and spread a thin layer of rice, leaving 1 inch uncovered at the top.

8) Arrange vegetable pieces in a horizontal line across the middle of the rice.

9) Using the mat, roll the nori tightly from the edge closest to you, sealing with water.

10) Repeat with remaining nori sheets and fillings. Use a sharp knife to slice each roll into 6-8 pieces, wiping the knife between cuts.

11) Arrange sushi rolls on a plate. Serve with soy sauce, pickled ginger, wasabi, and sesame seeds if desired. Enjoy!

Nutritional Value:

Calories: 350 kcal; Protein: 8g; Fat: 10g; Carbs: 60g; Fiber: 8g

Tuna and White Bean Salad

➤ **Prep Time:** 15mins
➤ **Cook Time:** No cooking
➤ **Servings:** 4

Ingredients:

- 2 cans (15oz each) of white beans (cannellini or great northern beans)
- 2 cans (5-6 ounces each) tuna packed in water, drained
- 1 small red onion, chopped
- 1 cup cherry tomatoes, halved
- 1 cucumber, diced
- 1 red bell pepper, diced
- 1/4 cup Kalamata olives

- 1/4 cup fresh parsley, chopped
- 1/4 cup fresh basil (optional)
- 2 tablespoons capers (optional)

For the Dressing:
- 1/4 cup extra-virgin olive oil
- 2 tablespoons lemon juice
- 1 tablespoon red wine vinegar
- 1 clove garlic, minced
- 1 teaspoon Dijon mustard
- Salt and pepper to taste

Procedures:

1) Drain and rinse white beans, place in a bowl, and add drained tuna, breaking it into chunks.
2) Finely chop red onion, halve cherry tomatoes, dice cucumber and red bell pepper, and halve Kalamata olives. Chop fresh parsley and basil (if using).
3) Whisk together olive oil, lemon juice, red wine vinegar, minced garlic, Dijon mustard, salt, and pepper in a small bowl.
4) Add chopped vegetables, herbs, and capers (if using) to the bowl with beans and tuna.
5) Pour dressing over the salad and toss gently to coat evenly.
6) Divide the salad among four plates or bowls and serve immediately. Enjoy!

Nutritional Value:

Calories: 400 kcal; Protein: 30g; Fat: 20g; Carbs: 30g; Fiber: 10g

Tomato Basil Soup with Grilled Cheese

➢ **Prep Time:** 15mins
➢ **Cook Time:** 30mins
➢ **Servings:** 4

Ingredients:

For the Tomato Basil Soup:
- 2 tablespoons olive oil
- 1 large onion, diced
- 3 cloves garlic, minced

- 2 cans (28oz each) of whole peeled tomatoes
- 2 cups vegetable broth
- 1/4 cup fresh basil leaves
- 1 teaspoon sugar (optional)
- Salt and pepper to taste
- half cup of coconut milk or heavy cream

For the Grilled Cheese:
- 8 slices of whole-grain or sourdough bread
- 4 tablespoons butter, softened
- 8 slices of cheddar cheese (or your favorite cheese)

Procedures:

1) Heat olive oil in a large pot over medium heat, cook diced onion until soft, then add minced garlic and cook until fragrant.
2) Combine whole peeled tomatoes, vegetable broth, and optional sugar. Boil well and let it simmer for 20 minutes.
3) Blend the soup with an immersion blender or in batches using a regular blender until smooth.
4) Stir in chopped basil leaves and heavy cream or coconut milk, season with salt and pepper, and simmer for 5 minutes.
5) Heat the skillet, butter the bread slices, and build sandwiches with cheese. Cook until the bread is golden and the cheese is melted.
6) Slice sandwiches diagonally. Ladle soup into bowls, garnish with basil, and serve with grilled cheese sandwiches. Enjoy!

Nutritional Value:

Calories: 600 kcal; Protein: 20g; Fat: 40g; Carbs: 50g; Fiber: 7g

6
Dinner Recipes

Baked Salmon with Asparagus

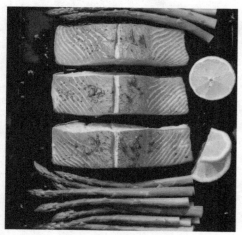

➤ **Prep Time:** 10mins
➤ **Cook Time:** 20mins
➤ **Servings:** 4

Ingredients:

- 4 salmon fillets (about 6oz each)
- 1 bunch asparagus, trimmed
- 2 tablespoons olive oil
- 1 lemon, thinly sliced
- 3 cloves garlic, minced
- 1 teaspoon dried dill or 1 tablespoon freshly chopped dill
- Salt and pepper to taste
- Lemon wedges, for serving
- Fresh parsley or dill for garnish

Procedures:

1) Set oven to 400°F (200°C) and line a baking sheet with parchment paper or foil.
2) Wash and trim asparagus, place on one side of the baking sheet, drizzle with olive oil, and season with minced garlic, salt, and pepper. Toss to coat.
3) Pat salmon fillets dry, place on the other side of the baking sheet, drizzle with olive oil, and season with dried dill, salt, and pepper. Garnish each fillet with a lemon slice.
4) Bake in the preheated oven for 15-20 minutes until the salmon is cooked through and the asparagus is tender.
5) Ensure that the salmon has an internal temperature of 145°F (63°C).
6) Let rest for a few minutes, then transfer to dishes. Garnish with fresh parsley or dill and serve with lemon wedges.

Nutritional Value:

Calories: 400 kcal; Protein: 35g; Fat: 25g; Carbs: 7g; Fiber: 3g

Zucchini Noodles with Pesto

➢ **Prep Time:** 15mins

➢ **Cook Time:** 5mins

➢ **Servings:** 4

Ingredients:

For the Zucchini Noodles:

- 4 medium zucchinis
- 1 tablespoon olive oil
- Salt and pepper to taste

For the Pesto:

- 2 cups fresh basil leaves
- Half a cup of finely grated Parmesan cheese (vegan option: use nutritional yeast)
- 1/3 cup pine nuts (or walnuts for a budget-friendly option)
- 2 cloves garlic
- 1/2 cup extra-virgin olive oil
- 1 tablespoon lemon juice
- Salt and pepper to taste

Optional Toppings:

Cherry tomatoes or Freshly grated Parmesan chees or Pine nuts or Walnuts or Red pepper flakes

Procedures:

1) Wash zucchinis, trim ends, and create noodles using a spiralizer, julienne peeler, or vegetable peeler. Place noodles in a colander, sprinkle with salt, and let sit for 10 minutes.

2) Garlic, pine nuts (or walnuts), grated Parmesan (or nutritional yeast), and basil leaves should all be combined in a food processor. Pulse until coarsely chopped. Slowly drizzle in olive oil until desired consistency is reached. Squeeze in the lemon juice and add the salt and pepper..

3) Heat olive oil in a skillet over medium heat, add zucchini noodles, and cook for 2-3 minutes until tender but crisp. Season with salt and pepper.

4) Remove skillet from heat, toss noodles with pesto until evenly coated. Divide among plates, top with halved cherry tomatoes, grated Parmesan, nuts, and red pepper flakes if desired. Serve immediately. Enjoy!

Nutritional Value:

Calories: 400 kcal; Protein: 10g;

Fat: 35g; Carbs: 15g; Fiber: 5g

Chicken and Broccoli Stir-Fry

➤ **Prep Time:** 15mins
➤ **Cook Time:** 15mins
➤ **Servings:** 4

Ingredients:

For the Stir-Fry:

- 1 pound of sliced, boneless, skinless chicken breasts
- 1 big broccoli head, divided into florets
- One thinly sliced red bell pepper (optional)
- 2 tablespoons vegetable oil (such as canola or sesame oil)
- 3 cloves garlic, minced
- 1 tablespoon ginger, minced
- 3 green onions

- 1/4 cup of tamari or low-sodium soy sauce (gluten-free)
- 2 tablespoons oyster sauce
- 1 tablespoon hoisin sauce
- 1 tablespoon cornstarch
- 1 tablespoon water
- 1 teaspoon sesame oil
- Cooked rice or noodles

Procedures:

1) Thinly slice chicken breasts, cut broccoli into florets, slice red bell pepper, mince garlic and ginger, and slice green onions, separating white and green parts.

2) Whisk together soy sauce, oyster sauce, hoisin sauce, cornstarch, water, and sesame oil in a small bowl.

3) Heat 1 tablespoon of vegetable oil in a skillet or wok over medium-high heat, cook chicken until browned and cooked through, then set aside.

4) In the same skillet, add remaining vegetable oil, then cook minced garlic, ginger, and white parts of green onions until fragrant.

5) Add broccoli florets and red bell pepper slices, stir-fry until tender-crisp. Return cooked chicken to the skillet.

6) Pour sauce over chicken and vegetables, stir to coat, and cook until sauce thickens.

7) Sprinkle green parts of green onions on top and serve over cooked rice or noodles. Enjoy!

Nutritional Value:

Calories: 350 kcal; Protein: 35g;

Fat: 15g; Carbs: 25g; Fiber: 4g

Creamy Garlic Chicken Breast

➢ **Prep Time:** 15mins
➢ **Cook Time:** 20mins
➢ **Servings:** 4

Ingredients:

For The Chicken:

- 2 to 3 big, skinless, boneless chicken breasts cut in half
- Four tablespoons of plain or all-purpose flour
- 4 tablespoons of freshly grated parmesan cheese
- 2 teaspoon salt
- 1 teaspoon garlic powder
- ½ teaspoon black pepper cracked

For The Sauce:

- 5 tablespoons olive oil
- 2 tablespoons butter
- 1 small onion finely chopped
- 1 head of garlic, peeled and cut into 10 to 12 pieces
- 1 ¼ cup chicken broth (stock)
- 1 ¼ cup heavy cream half and half (or evaporated milk)
- half cup of freshly grated parmesan cheese
- 2 tablespoons fresh parsley to serve

Instructions

1) Season chicken with salt, garlic powder, and pepper.
2) Combine flour and Parmesan cheese in a bowl, dredge chicken in mixture, and shake off excess.
3) Heat oil and butter in a skillet over medium-high heat, fry chicken until golden and cooked through. Transfer to a warm plate.
4) Wipe skillet, add more oil and butter, cook remaining chicken, and transfer to the same plate.

5) Reduce heat to medium, sauté onion in the remaining oil until softened.

6) Smash garlic cloves, add to the pan with more oil, and sauté until fragrant. Add broth, scrape up browned bits, and simmer until reduced by half.

7) Reduce heat to medium-low, add cream, and simmer for 2-3 minutes. Mix in Parmesan cheese, cook until melted, and season with salt and pepper.

8) Add chicken back to the pan, simmer for 2-3 minutes to thicken sauce.

9) Garnish with parsley and black pepper. Serve over pasta, cauliflower mash, zucchini noodles, rice, or mashed potatoes. Enjoy!

Nutritional Value:

Calories: 666 kcal; Carbs: 11g; Protein: 22g; Fat: 60g; Fiber: 1g

Black Bean and Sweet Potato Tacos

➤ **Prep Time:** 15mins
➤ **Cook Time:** 30mins
➤ **Servings:** 8 Tacos

Ingredients:

For the Roasted Sweet Potatoes:

- 2 large sweet potatoes
- 2 tablespoons olive oil
- 1 teaspoon ground cumin
- 1 teaspoon smoked paprika
- 1/2 teaspoon chili powder
- 1/2 teaspoon garlic powder
- Salt and pepper to taste

For the Black Beans:

- 1 can (15 ounces) black beans
- 1 tablespoon olive oil
- 1 small onion, diced

- 2 cloves garlic, minced
- 1 teaspoon ground cumin
- 1/2 teaspoon smoked paprika
- Salt and pepper to taste

For the Tacos:
- 8 small corn or whole-wheat tortillas
- 1 avocado, sliced
- 1 cup cherry tomatoes, halved
- 1/2 cup red onion, chopped
- 1/4 cup fresh cilantro, chopped
- 1/4 cup crumbled feta or cotija cheese (optional)
- Lime wedges, for serving

Procedures:

1) Set oven to 425°F (220°C) and line a baking sheet with parchment paper or foil.
2) Toss diced sweet potatoes with olive oil and spices, spread on the baking sheet, and roast for 25-30 minutes, stirring halfway.
3) Heat olive oil in a skillet over medium heat, cook diced onion until soft, add minced garlic until fragrant. Stir in the spices and black beans, then allow it to cook well.
4) Heat tortillas over a gas flame or in a dry skillet until pliable.
5) Place roasted sweet potatoes and black beans on each tortilla, top with avocado slices, cherry tomatoes, red onion, cilantro, and optional crumbled cheese.
6) Serve tacos with lime wedges. Enjoy!

Nutritional Value:
Calories: 400 kcal; Protein: 12g; Fat: 18g; Carbs: 50g; Fiber: 15g

Quinoa and Veggie Stuffed Acorn Squash

➤ **Prep Time:** 15mins
➤ **Cook Time:** 60mins
➤ **Servings:** 4

Ingredients:

For the Acorn Squash:
- 2 medium acorn squashes
- 2 tablespoons olive oil
- Salt and pepper to taste

For the Quinoa & Veggie Filling:
- 1 cup quinoa, rinsed
- 2 cups vegetable broth or water
- 1 tablespoon olive oil
- 1 small onion, diced
- 2 cloves garlic, minced
- 1 red bell pepper, diced
- 1 zucchini, diced
- 1 carrot, diced
- 1 cup baby spinach, chopped
- 1/4 cup dried cranberries
- 1/4 cup chopped pecans or walnuts
- 1 teaspoon dried thyme
- 1 teaspoon dried oregano
- 1/2 teaspoon ground cumin
- Salt and pepper to taste
- 1/4 cup crumbled feta cheese
- Fresh parsley for garnish

Procedures:

1) Set oven to 400°F (200°C). Cut acorn squashes in half, scoop out seeds, brush with olive oil, and season with salt and pepper.

2) Place squash halves cut side down on a baking sheet and roast for 30-40 minutes until tender.

3) Combine rinsed quinoa and vegetable broth (or water) in a saucepan, bring to a boil, then simmer until tender. Fluff with a fork.

83

4) Heat olive oil in a skillet, cook diced onion until soft, add minced garlic, then add diced red bell pepper, zucchini, and carrot. Cook until tender.

5) Stir in chopped spinach until wilted, then add cooked quinoa, dried cranberries, chopped nuts, dried thyme, dried oregano, ground cumin, salt, and pepper. Cook until heated through.

6) Fill roasted squash halves with the quinoa and veggie mixture, pressing lightly. Optionally, sprinkle with crumbled feta cheese.

7) Return stuffed squash to the oven and bake for an additional 10-15 minutes until heated through and lightly browned.

8) Let cool, garnish with fresh parsley if desired, and serve warm. Enjoy!

Nutritional Value:

Calories: 450 kcal; Protein: 12g;

Fat: 20g; Carbs: 65g; Fiber: 12g

Turkey Meatballs with Spaghetti Squash

➤ **Prep Time:** 20mins
➤ **Cook Time:** 60mins
➤ **Servings:** 4

Ingredients:

For the Spaghetti Squash:
- 1 large spaghetti squash
- 2 tablespoons olive oil
- Salt and pepper to taste

For the Turkey Meatballs:
- 1 pound ground turkey
- 1/4 cup grated Parmesan cheese
- 1/4 cup of gluten-free or whole-wheat breadcrumbs
- 1 large egg
- 2 cloves garlic, minced
- 1 small onion, finely chopped

- 1/4 cup fresh parsley, chopped
- 1 teaspoon dried oregano
- 1 teaspoon dried basil
- Salt and pepper to taste
- 2 tablespoons olive oil

For the Marinara Sauce:

- 2 tablespoons olive oil
- 1 small onion, finely chopped
- 3 cloves garlic, minced
- 1 can (28oz) crushed tomatoes
- 1 teaspoon dried oregano
- 1 teaspoon dried basil
- Salt and pepper to taste
- Fresh basil or parsley for garnish

Procedures:

1) Set oven to 400°F (200°C). Cut acorn squashes in half, scoop out seeds, brush with olive oil, and season with salt and pepper.

2) Place squash halves cut side down on a baking sheet and roast for 30-40 minutes until tender.

3) Combine rinsed quinoa and vegetable broth (or water) in a saucepan, bring to a boil, then simmer until tender. Fluff with a fork.

4) Heat olive oil in a skillet, cook diced onion until soft, add minced garlic, then add diced red bell pepper, zucchini, and carrot. Cook until tender.

5) Stir in chopped spinach until wilted, then add cooked quinoa, dried cranberries, chopped nuts, dried thyme, dried oregano, ground cumin, salt, and pepper. Cook until heated through.

6) Fill roasted squash halves with the quinoa and veggie mixture, pressing lightly. Optionally, sprinkle with crumbled feta cheese.

7) Return stuffed squash to the oven and bake for an additional 10-15 minutes until heated through and lightly browned.

8) Let cool, garnish with fresh parsley if desired, and serve warm. Enjoy!

Nutritional Value:

Calories: 450 kcal; Protein: 35g; Fat: 25g; Carbs: 30g; Fiber: 7g

Eggplant Parmesan

➤ **Prep Time:** 30mins
➤ **Cook Time:** 50mins
➤ **Servings:** 4

Ingredients:

For the Eggplant:
- 2 large eggplants
- 1 tablespoon salt
- 2 cups breadcrumbs (whole wheat or gluten-free)
- 1/2 cup grated Parmesan cheese
- 1 teaspoon dried oregano
- 1 teaspoon dried basil
- 1/2 teaspoon garlic powder
- 2 large eggs
- 1/2 cup milk (dairy or non-dairy)
- 1/2 cup flour (all-purpose or gluten-free)
- 1/4 cup olive oil (for frying)

For the Marinara Sauce:
- 2 tablespoons olive oil
- 1 small onion, finely chopped
- 3 cloves garlic, minced
- 1 can (28oz) crushed tomatoes
- 1 teaspoon dried oregano
- 1 teaspoon dried basil
- 1/2 teaspoon red pepper flakes (optional)
- Salt and pepper to taste

For Assembling:
- 2 cups shredded mozzarella cheese
- 1/2 cup grated Parmesan cheese
- Fresh basil leaves for garnish

Procedures:

1) Slice eggplants into rounds, salt both sides, and let sit for 30 minutes on a paper towel-lined baking sheet. Rinse and pat dry.

2) Mix breadcrumbs, Parmesan, oregano, basil, and garlic powder in one bowl. Stir the

milk and eggs in a separate bowl. Place flour in a third bowl.

3) Dredge eggplant slices in flour, dip in egg mixture, then coat with breadcrumb mixture.

4) Heat olive oil in a skillet and fry eggplant slices until golden brown and crispy. Drain on paper towels.

5) Sauté onion in olive oil until soft, add garlic, then stir in crushed tomatoes, oregano, basil, red pepper flakes, salt, and pepper. Simmer for 15-20 minutes.

6) Preheat oven to 375°F (190°C). Spread marinara sauce in a baking dish, layer with fried eggplant, more sauce, mozzarella, and Parmesan. Continue layering to finish the cheese and sauce.

7) Bake for 20 minutes while covered with foil. Remove foil and bake for an additional 15-20 minutes until cheese is melted and bubbly.

8) Let cool, garnish with fresh basil, and serve warm with pasta, garlic bread, or salad. Enjoy!

Nutritional Value:

Calories: 550 kcal; Protein: 25g;

Fat: 35g; Carbs: 45g; Fiber: 9g

Shrimp and Vegetable Skewers

➤ **Prep Time:** 30mins
➤ **Cook Time:** 15mins
➤ **Servings:** 8 Skewers

Ingredients:

- 1 pound large shrimp, peeled

- 1 red bell pepper, sliced into 1-inch chunks
- 1 yellow bell pepper, chopped into 1-inch slices
- 1 zucchini, sliced into 1/2-inch rounds
- 1 red onion, cut into wedges
- 8 ounces mushrooms, halved
- 2 tablespoons olive oil
- 2 tablespoons lemon juice
- 3 cloves garlic, minced
- 1 teaspoon dried oregano
- 1 teaspoon dried basil
- 1/2 teaspoon smoked paprika
- Salt and pepper to taste
- Fresh parsley or cilantro
- Lemon wedges for serving (optional)

Procedures:

1) Mix olive oil, lemon juice, minced garlic, dried basil, dried oregano, smoked paprika, salt, and pepper in a big bowl.

2) Add shrimp to the marinade, toss to coat, cover, and refrigerate for 15 minutes.

3) Toss bell peppers, zucchini, red onion, and mushrooms with some of the shrimp marinade in another bowl. Let marinate for 15 minutes.

4) Soak wooden skewers in water for at least 30 minutes if using.

5) Thread marinated shrimp and vegetables onto the skewers, alternating between shrimp and vegetables.

6) Heat grill to medium-high (375-400°F or 190-200°C) and lightly oil the grates.

7) Cook skewers for about 2-3 minutes per side until shrimp are pink and opaque and vegetables are tender and slightly charred, about 10-15 minutes total.

8) Let skewers rest briefly, garnish with parsley or cilantro, and serve with lemon wedges. Enjoy!

Nutritional Value:

Calories: 300 kcal; Protein: 30g; Fat: 12g; Carbs: 15g; Fiber: 4g

Melt In Your Mouth (MIYM) Chicken Breasts

➢ **Prep Time:** 5mins
➢ **Cook Time:** 25mins
➢ **Servings:** 8

Ingredients

- 1 cup sour cream
- 2 teaspoons garlic powder
- 1 teaspoon seasoned salt
- 1/2 teaspoon fresh ground black pepper
- 1 and a half cups of shredded Parmesan cheese
- Three pounds of boneless chicken breasts, trimmed of extra fat.

Instructions:

1) Set oven to 375°F and lightly coat a 9×13 baking dish with nonstick spray.
2) In a medium bowl, mix together sour cream, garlic powder, seasoned salt, pepper, and 1 cup of Parmesan cheese.
3) Place chicken breasts evenly in the baking dish. Spread sour cream mixture on top and sprinkle with remaining Parmesan cheese.
4) Bake for 25-30 minutes until chicken is cooked through. Turn oven to broil and broil for 2-3 minutes until lightly browned on top. Serve immediately.

Nutritional Value:

Calories: 321 kal; Fat: 13g;
Carbs: 3g; Protein: 46g

Conclusion

Your journey with the Epi Diet has been a path of discovery, growth, and transformation. From learning about nutrient-dense foods to preparing delicious and healthy meals, you've embraced a lifestyle that nurtures your body and soul. Now, as you continue on this journey, it's essential to focus on maintaining the habits and principles that have brought you to this point.

Maintaining the Epi Diet isn't just about sticking to a set of rules or guidelines. It's about adopting a lifestyle that puts your health first. It's about making choices that support your health, energy, and happiness every day. This journey is a lifelong commitment to yourself, and it's filled with opportunities to learn, grow, and thrive.

Embrace Whole Foods:

The foundation of the Epi Diet is built on whole, unprocessed foods. Continue to fill your plate with colorful vegetables, fresh fruits, lean proteins, whole grains, and healthy fats. These foods are rich in the nutrients your body needs to function at its best. They provide you with energy, boost your immune system, and keep your mind active.

Plan and Prepare:

One of the keys to maintaining the Epi Diet is planning and preparation. Set up time every week to organize your snacks and meals. This helps you stay on track and avoid the temptation of unhealthy options. Prepare meals in advance, so you always have something nutritious to eat, even on your busiest days. Planning and preparation make it easier to make healthy choices consistently.

Stay Hydrated:

Every bodily function requires the presence of water. Make it a daily practice to drink a lot of water. Hydration supports digestion, keeps your skin healthy, and helps you feel energized. Always have a bottle of water with you, and use it often. Herbal teas and infusions can also contribute to your hydration needs.

Listen to Your Body:

Your body is intelligent and knows exactly what it needs. Pay attention to hunger and fullness cues. When you are hungry, eat, and when you are satisfied, stop. This mindful approach to eating helps you stay in tune with your body's needs and prevents overeating. It's critical to respect your body's signals and believe that it knows what's best for you.

Find Joy in Movement:

Physical activity is a vital part of the Epi Diet lifestyle. Find activities you enjoy and incorporate them into your daily schedule. Whether it's walking, dancing, swimming, or yoga, moving your body helps you feel strong and alive. Exercise supports your physical health, boosts your mood, and reduces stress. Make movement a fun and important part of your life.

Celebrate Your Progress:

Take the time to celebrate your accomplishments, no matter how minor they may appear. Every step you take toward maintaining the Epi Diet is a victory. Consider how far you have come and acknowledge the positive improvements you've implemented. Celebrating your accomplishments reaffirms your dedication and keeps you inspired to continue.

Be Kind to Yourself:

There will be times when you face challenges or slip up. Remember that it's okay to make mistakes. Be kind and compassionate to yourself. Instead of dwelling on setbacks, focus on how you can get back on track. Learn from your experiences and turn them into chances for growth. Self-compassion is a powerful tool for maintaining a healthy lifestyle.

Adapt and Adjust:

Life is full of changes and challenges. Be adaptable and open to change your diet and lifestyle as necessary. There may be times when you need to make adjustments to your routine or try new strategies. Accept change as a chance for growth and learning. Being adaptable helps you stay resilient and committed to your health journey.

Success Stories

Success stories are powerful reminders of the transformative impact of the Epi Diet. They are real-life examples of how embracing a healthier lifestyle can change lives in profound ways. These stories are filled with emotion, triumph, and personal growth, offering inspiration and hope to you on your journey. Here are some success stories from people who have experienced the benefits of the Epi Diet.

Sarah's Story: Finding Energy and Joy

Sarah had struggled with fatigue and low energy for years. She often felt sluggish and found it hard to get through the day without multiple cups of coffee. When she discovered the Epi Diet, she decided to give it a try, hoping it might help her feel better.

"*I was skeptical at first, but I was desperate for a change,*" Sarah says. "*I started by incorporating more whole foods into my diet and cutting out processed foods. Within a few weeks, I noticed a significant difference in my energy levels. I no longer needed that afternoon coffee to stay awake.*"

Sarah's transformation didn't stop there. As she continued to follow the Epi Diet, she found that her mood improved, and she felt more joyful and positive. "*I can't believe how much better I feel. I have the energy to play with my kids, go for walks, and enjoy life. The Epi Diet has truly changed my life for the better.*"

John's Story: Overcoming Health Challenges

John had been diagnosed with high blood pressure and was at risk for diabetes. His doctor had warned him that he needed to make significant lifestyle changes to improve his health. Feeling overwhelmed, John turned to the Epi Diet for guidance.

"*I was scared when my doctor told me about my health issues,*" John recalls. "*I knew I had to make changes, but I didn't know where to start. The Epi Diet gave me a clear path to follow.*"

John began by focusing on nutrient-dense foods and cutting out sugary drinks and snacks. He also started walking every day. Within a few months, John's blood pressure had dropped, and his blood sugar levels were stable.

"My doctor was amazed at my progress," John says with pride. "I feel healthier and more alive than I have in years. The Epi Diet showed me that it's never too late to take control of my health."

Maria's Story: Embracing Self-Love and Confidence

Maria had battled her weight and self-esteem for a long time. She had tried numerous diets, but nothing seemed to work long-term. She often felt defeated and unhappy with her body. When she learned about the Epi Diet, she decided to give it one more try, hoping for a different outcome.

"The Epi Diet was different from anything I'd tried before," Maria explains. "It wasn't just about losing weight; it was about nourishing my body and loving myself."

As Maria embraced the principles of the Epi Diet, she began to see changes. She lost weight gradually and healthily, but more importantly, she started to feel confident and proud of herself.

"I realized that my worth isn't determined by a number on the scale. The Epi Diet taught me to appreciate my body for all that it does."

Maria now feels empowered and confident in her own skin.

"I love the person I've become. I'm healthier, happier, and more self-assured. The Epi Diet helped me find the self-love and confidence I had been searching for."

David's Story: Building a Healthier Family

David was concerned about his family's eating habits. With two young children, he wanted to set a good example and ensure they grew up with a healthy relationship with food. He introduced the Epi Diet to his family, hoping to make positive changes together.

"It wasn't easy at first," David admits. "We had to make some significant changes to our meals and snacks. But we did it together as a family, and that made all the difference."

David's family began cooking meals together, incorporating more vegetables, fruits, and whole grains into their diet. They also started enjoying outdoor activities like hiking and biking. "We became more active and connected as a family," David says. "My kids learned to love healthy foods and enjoy being active."

The changes paid off. David noticed that his children had more energy, were less prone to illness, and were happier overall.

"The Epi Diet brought us closer as a family and helped us build healthier habits. I'm grateful for the positive impact it's had on our lives."

These successes are a handful of the Epi Diet's remarkable ability to change lives. They remind us that with dedication, support, and the right approach, we can achieve our health and wellness goals. Each person's journey is unique, but the principles of the Epi Diet provide a solid foundation for a healthier, happier life.

I wrote this book with the sole purpose of exceeding your expectations. If you don't mind, please share your experience for other shoppers to see. Your feedback would be greatly appreciated.

Made in the USA
Las Vegas, NV
12 October 2024